W.C. FIELDS
SPEAKS

PRICE/STERN/SLOAN
Publishers, Inc., Los Angeles
1981

FIRST PRINTING – FEBRUARY 1981

Copyright© 1981 by W.C. Fields Productions, Inc.
Published by Price/Stern/Sloan Publishers, Inc.
410 North La Cienega Boulevard, Los Angeles, California 90048

ISBN: 0-8431-0392-2

CONTENTS

Introduction

It's a great tribute to W.C. Fields' talent that his irascible humor is as popular today as it was fifty years ago. What sets this vaudeville juggler, comedian, and movie great apart from his contemporaries is the Fields penchant for sharp, irreverent comments delivered in a unique style. His quotes have become famous, perhaps, because they mirror our own attitudes.

The quotes herein provide a timeless testimony to Fields' wonderfully outrageous humor - made all the more remarkable by the fact that he needed no writers to make him witty.

This volume presents the best of W.C. Fields. You'll find his cantankerous comments as well as the more weightful remarks that provide an insight into the warm, hidden side of this complex man. Also included are numerous photos of The Great One - some of them rare, behind-the-scenes glimpses.

Fractured Philosophy

"Let me give you one word of fatherly advice ... never give a sucker an even break."

"Even the one or two honest men living wouldn't hesitate to steal when thirsty."

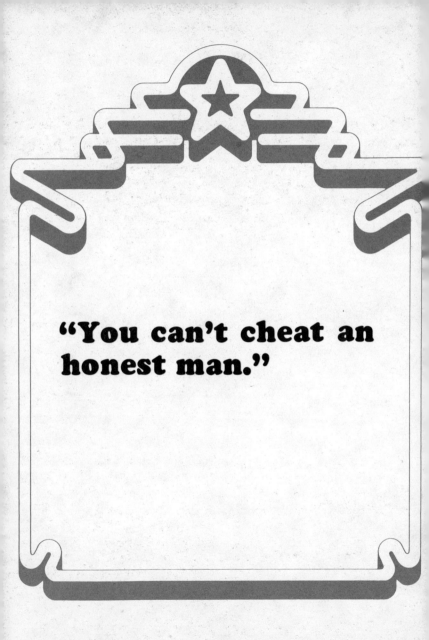

"You can't cheat an honest man."

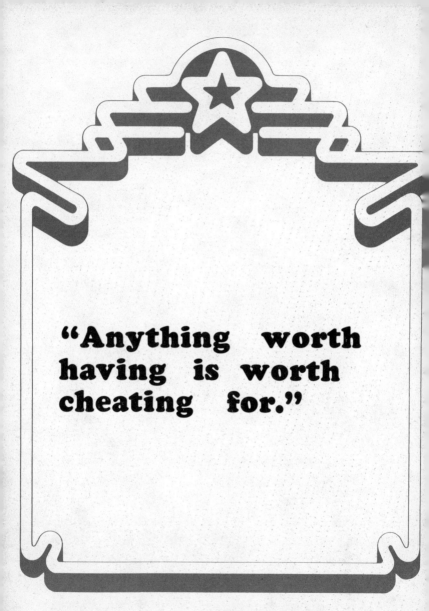

"Anything worth having is worth cheating for."

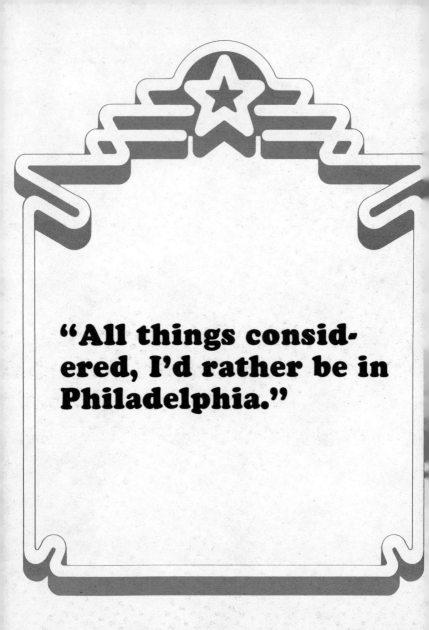

"All things considered, I'd rather be in Philadelphia."

On Women

"Hello, my turtle-dove. Now that I'm here I'll dally in the valley . . . and believe me I can dally."

"Marriage is a two-way proposition, but never let the woman know she is one of the ways."

"I was in love with a
beautiful blonde once:
she drove me to drink;
it's the one thing I'm
indebted to her for."

"Women are like elephants to me; they're nice to look at but I wouldn't want to own one."

"The nation needs to return to the colonial trend of life, when a wife was judged by the amount of wood she could split."

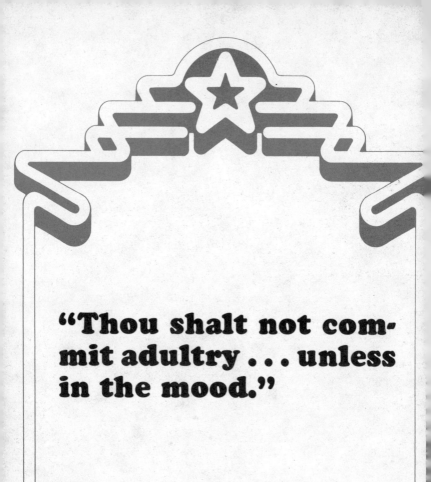

"Thou shalt not commit adultry . . . unless in the mood."

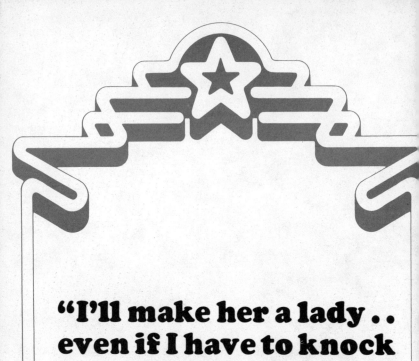

"I'll make her a lady ..
even if I have to knock
her down to do it."

"Is she one of a kind or part of a matched set?"

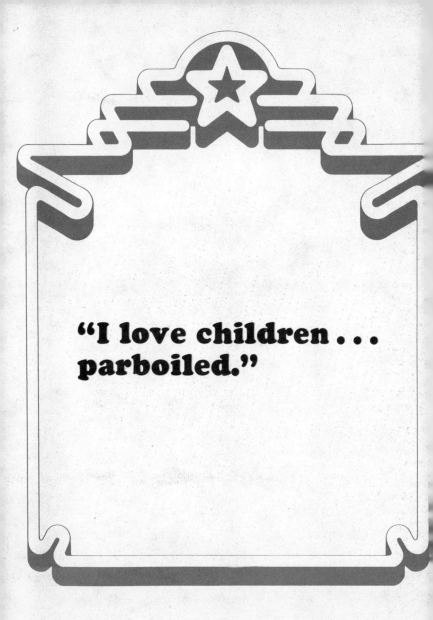

"I love children . . .
parboiled."

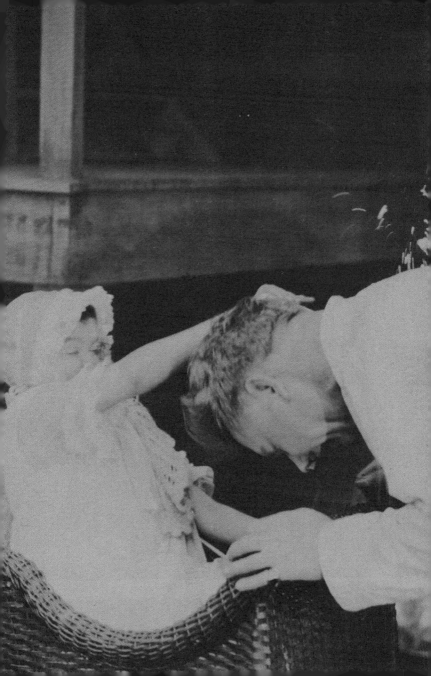

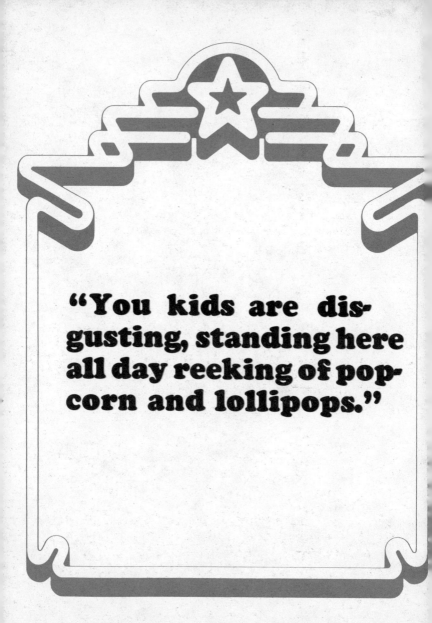

"You kids are disgusting, standing here all day reeking of popcorn and lollipops."

34

"Political baby-kissing must come to an end unless the size and age of the babies be materially increased."

"There's not a man in America who at one time or another hasn't had a secret desire to boot a child in the ass."

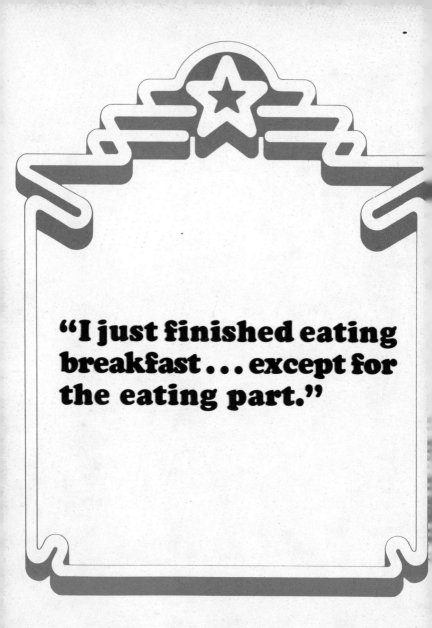

"I just finished eating breakfast . . . except for the eating part."

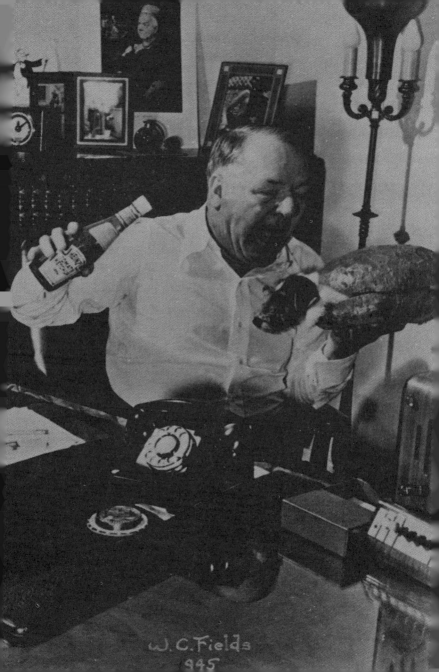

W. C. Fields
1945

"A dog knows a tramp
when he sniffs one."

42

"I have not changed
my position about
either whiskey or
dogs. As always, I
am in favor of one,
against the other."

On Drinking

"Never trust a man who doesn't drink."

"A wonderful drink, wine . . . did you ever hear of a barefooted Italian grape crusher with athlete's foot?"

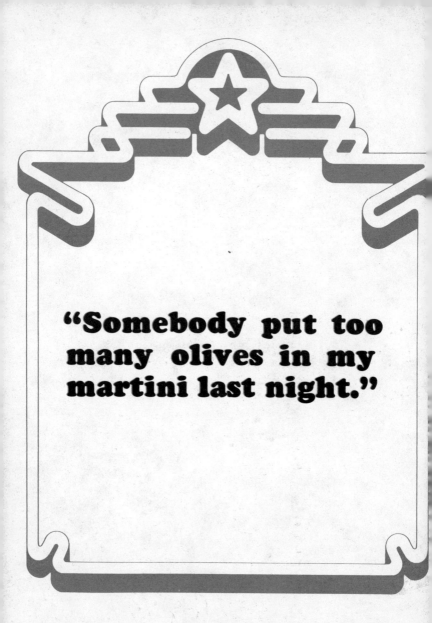

"Somebody put too many olives in my martini last night."

"I never drink water
because fish f... in it."

"All roads lead to rum."

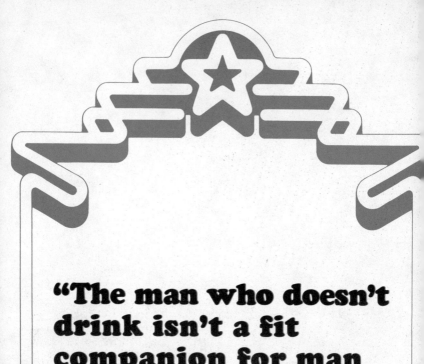

"The man who doesn't drink isn't a fit companion for man or beast."

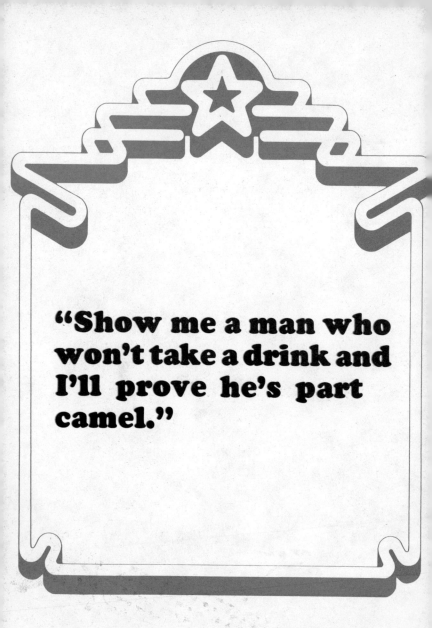

"Show me a man who won't take a drink and I'll prove he's part camel."

"I've been asked if I ever get the D.T.'s. I don't know; it's hard to tell where Hollywood ends and the D.T.'s begin."

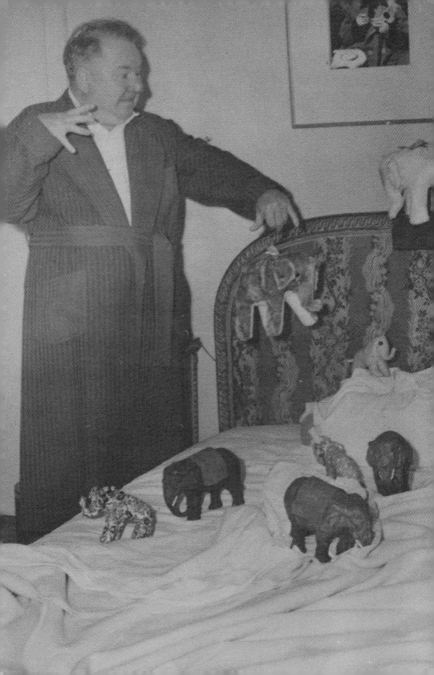

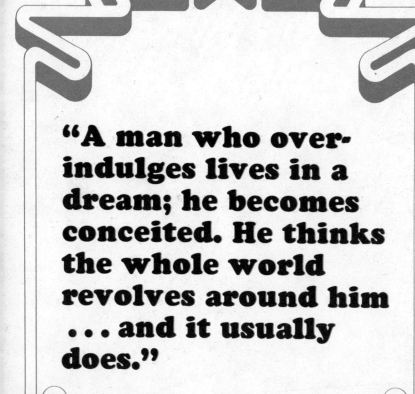

"A man who over-indulges lives in a dream; he becomes conceited. He thinks the whole world revolves around him ... and it usually does."

"The laziest man I ever met put popcorn in his pancakes so they would turn over by themselves."

"Every cloud has a silver lining and every plate of vegetable soup is filled with vegetables."

"Many times I have felt I was alone, crying in the wilderness—an arid wilderness populated by sagebrush, bluenoses, and dogs."

"I haven't been sick a single day since I had T.B. as a boy. A steady diet of cigars and whiskey cured me."

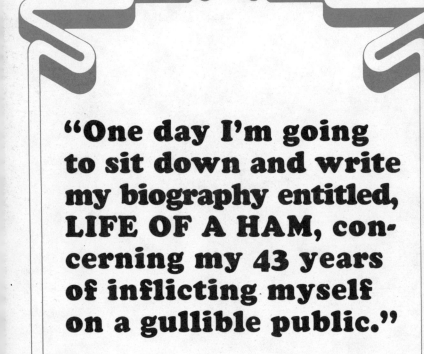

"One day I'm going to sit down and write my biography entitled, LIFE OF A HAM, concerning my 43 years of inflicting myself on a gullible public."

"Anyone who hates children and dogs can't be all bad."

"Most people have a feeling they are going to be reincarnated and come back to this life. Not me. I know I'm going through here only once."

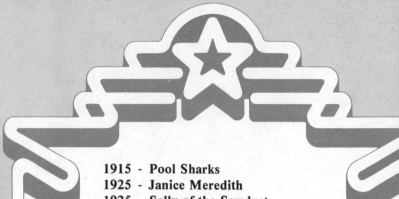

1915 - Pool Sharks
1925 - Janice Meredith
1925 - Sally of the Sawdust
1926 - It's the Old Army Game
1926 - That Royle Girl
1926 - So's Your Old Man
1927 - Running Wild
1927 - Two Flaming Youths
1927 - The Potters
1928 - Tillie's Punctured Romance
1928 - Fools for Luck
1930 - The Golf Specialist
1930 - Her Majesty Love
1932 - The Dentist
1932 - If I Had a Million
1932 - Million Dollar Legs
1932 - International House
1933 - The Barber Shop
1933 - The Fatal Glass of Beer
1933 - The Pharmacist

The Films of W.C. Fields

1933 - Alice in Wonderland
1933 - Tillie and Gus
1934 - Six of a Kind
1934 - You're Telling Me
1934 - Mrs. Wiggs of the Cabbage Patch
1934 - It's a Gift
1934 - The Old-Fashioned Way
1935 - Mississippi
1935 - The Man on the Flying Trapeze
1935 - David Copperfield
1936 - Poppy
1938 - The Big Broadcast of 1938
1939 - You Can't Cheat an Honest Man
1940 - The Bank Dick
1940 - My Little Chickadee
1941 - Never Give a Sucker an Even Break
1942 - Tales of Manhatten
1944 - Follow the Boys
1944 - Song of the Open Road
1945 - Sensations of 1945

The Films of W.C. Fields